First published in 2025 by Rock Point, an imprint of The Quarto Group,
142 West 36th Street, 4th Floor, New York, NY 10018, USA
(212) 779-4972 www.Quarto.com

Rock Point titles are also available at discount for retail, wholesale, promotional, and bulk purchase. For details, contact the Special Sales Manager by email at specialsales@quarto.com or by mail at The Quarto Group, Attn: Special Sales Manager, 100 Cummings Center Suite 265D, Beverly, MA 01915 USA.

10 9 8 7 6 5 4 3 2 1

ISBN: 978-1-57715-504-1

Digital edition published in 2025
eISBN: 978-0-7603-9407-6

Group Publisher: Rage Kindelsperger
Editorial Director: Erin Canning
Creative Director: Laura Drew
Managing Editor: Cara Donaldson
Editor: Nicole James
Text: Sara Weiss
Cover and Interior Illustrations: Alan Baker
Cover and Interior Design: Evelin Kasikov

Library of Congress Cataloging-in-Publication Da

Names: Weiss, Sara (Writing consultant), author.
Title: A labrador life : what to know and love abo
the labrador retriever / by Sara Weiss.
Description: New York : Rock Point, 2025. |
Includes bibliographical references. | Summary
"A Labrador Life is a gorgeously illustrated
guide to Labrador retrievers that explores the
breed's loveable traits and provides helpful
tips for every owner"-- Provided by publisher.
Identifiers: LCCN 2024041813 (print) | LCCN
2024041814 (ebook) | ISBN
9781577155041 (hardcover) | ISBN
9780760394076 (ebook)
Subjects: LCSH: Labrador retriever--Popular
works. | Labrador retriever--Pictorial works.
Classification: LCC SF429.L3 W448 2025 (print) |
LCC SF429.L3 (ebook) | DDC 636.752/7--dc23
eng/20241029
LC record available at https://lccn.loc.
gov/2024041813
LC ebook record available at https://lccn.loc.
gov/2024041814

Printed in China

A LABRADOR LIFE

What to Know and Love about
the Labrador Retriever

Sara Weiss

ROCK
POINT

Dedication

To Mom and Dad

Introduction 9

Friendliness 15

Empathy 25

Family Friends 37

Smarties 47

Duck Hunters 57

Eating Machines 71

At Your Service 81

Outdoorsmen 91

Affection 103

Finding the Perfect Name for Your Labrador Retriever 118

Taking Care of Your Labrador 120

Labrador Resources 124

Acknowledgments 126

About the Author 127

Introduction

Labrador retrievers are one of the most popular dog breeds in the world. From 1991 to 2022, they had a thirty-one-year reign as the most popular dog breed in America. (French bulldogs took the lead after that.) Friendly and playful, athletic and outdoorsy, kind, empathetic, and reliable, Labradors make the perfect pets.

Although Labradors are named after a region in Canada called, well, *Labrador*, they actually originate from the nearby island of Newfoundland. The ancestors of the modern retriever were called St. John's water dogs (a variant of the breed that has since gone extinct). Another name for these water dogs was "the lesser Newfoundlands" (this might sound kind of like an insult, but hopefully our Labradors don't mind).

These water dogs were mostly black with tuxedo markings on their faces, chest, and legs, and they were a favorite among fisherman for their working behavior and their love of the water. They loved to dive, swim, and retrieve, and their water-resistant short hair prevented ice from getting stuck to their coats.

Along their journey from Canadian hunting dog to a household name, Labs made a pit stop in Britain's royal kennels. In England in the 1800s, the Earl of Malmesbury sought out St. John's water dogs for duck hunting on his estate. He imported the dogs from Newfoundland to England and began a breeding program, carried on by the second and third Earls of Malmesbury. The kennels of the Dukes of Buccleuch (dare you to say these names three times fast!) were also instrumental in the growth of the breed's popularity. These noble families helped to propagate breeding programs that led to the creation of our lovable Labs.

As a part of this noble mission, St. John's water dogs were crossbred with other dogs to create retrievers, including the flat-coated retriever, the curly-coated retriever, the Chesapeake Bay retriever, the golden retriever, and the Labrador retriever. They were also ancestors to the modern Newfoundland breed.

These "gun dogs" or "bird dogs" were known for chasing and catching prey with a "soft mouth" so they could deliver prey intact. The breed originally had black coats, but later, the mixture of other bloodlines led to the creation of chocolate and yellow Labs.

Today, Labrador retrievers still have short hair and dense, water-resistant coats. They come in three colors: black, chocolate, and yellow.

They are generally 21–24 inches (53–61 cm) tall, they weigh about 55–80 pounds (25–36 kg), and they live for an average of 13 years. They have broad heads with expressive eyebrows, soft ears that lay close to their heads, kind eyes that can be hazel or brown, a strong jaw with a graceful curve, and a powerful and muscular body. They are ideal sporting dogs, but they have also come to be our best companions, providing comfort and bringing us an endless amount of joy. Their intelligence, trainability, and reliability also make them wonderful service, therapy, and guide dogs.

In fact, Labs have a storied history of saving lives. Swansea Jack, a black Labrador from Wales in the 1930s, is reported to have saved twenty-seven people from drowning in a river, including a twelve-year-old boy. In 1936, he was awarded the "Bravest Dog of the Year" award by the *Star* newspaper in London.

Many more Lab heroes have since followed in his footsteps. Two yellow Labs named Salty and Roselle led their owners out of the World Trade Center on September 11, 2001, before the towers collapsed. The guide dogs navigated their way down more than seventy-one flights of stairs, escorting their owners to safety. Organizations such as Hero Labradors specialize in training Labradors to help disabled veterans and first responders, a testament to the grit, intelligence, and bravery of these incredible dogs.

If you are thinking about bringing a Labrador into your home, there are a few things you should keep in mind. While they are low maintenance when it comes to temperament, grooming, and training, they do need a lot of mental stimulation and exercise to stay happy, healthy, and engaged. They are prone to certain health issues such as hip and elbow dysplasia, eye diseases, exercise-induced collapse, and obesity (and they might try to eat anything and everything, so dog-proofing will be necessary). You'll want to feed them a high-quality, age-appropriate diet; make sure to get them plenty of exercise; take them to the vet for regular visits; and of course, give them all the love. With routine health checks and lots of care, Labrador retrievers can live a lifetime of happiness.

And happiness is what they're all about. With the athleticism and energy of their sporting past combined with their confident friendliness, they offer a wonderful mix of characteristics that make them the ideal dog. When it comes down to it, Labradors are perfection, full of boisterous energy and a joy for living. They love to show affection to their favorite people and greet everyone they meet with a warm welcome. Their intuitive and empathetic nature brings us comfort when we need it most. Their wagging tails, smiling faces, and kind eyes make us feel loved. They are our loyal friends, our companions, our service dogs, our hiking buds, our snuggle muffins, our furry friends—our Labradors.

FRIENDLINESS

If someone tells you that you have **Labrador energy,** it means you are **super confident, excitable, friendly** to everyone, and at times . . . okay, a little much. There is no one happier to see you than a Labrador. It doesn't matter if you've only been gone for fifteen minutes to pick up a pack of gum; when you return home, your Labrador will greet you like you're Tom Hanks at the end of *Cast Away*.

When they see you, they will not only wag their tail; **they will shimmy their whole rear.** They will barrel through the room and skitter around with an abundance of joy, knocking down anything in their way. They will sniff you, lick you, jump up on you, bring you a toy, and generally do anything they can to let you know **just how very much you have been missed.** Yes, they will give the same kind of welcome to the meter reader from the water company, but don't let that bother you.

No Pretenses

Some dogs make you work for it. They can be independent, aloof, and withholding of affection. When you come home and your dog can't even be bothered to lift their snout from their paws, it makes you wonder, does my dog love me, or am I just a kibble sugar daddy to them?

This is not a concern you will have with a Labrador. There's no wondering if they are "just not that into you." They will make it crystal clear: "I am so into you." No games. No playing hard to get. They will not try to tame their excitement when you walk into the room. They will smother you with affection. It's lovely to be with a creature who so obviously values you and wants to be around you—and of course, the feeling is mutual.

Welcome!

True, they are also *into* your partner, your great aunt, your neighbor, the mailman, the exterminator, and the burglar who has just climbed in through your window. These people will also receive an ecstatic, warm welcome from your Labrador when they come to your home. Labradors can certainly be trained to be good watchdogs because of their natural tendency to be loyal, alert, and protective of their loved ones, but on the whole, they are usually very friendly to family and strangers alike.

Happy Signs

It's no secret when your Lab is happy to see you, but here are some obvious signs to let you know.

Smiles
When Labradors smile with open, happy mouths, it shows they are comfortable and relaxed.

Tongue out
Again, your Lab is mostly relaxed and content when they let their tongue hang out of their mouths, sometimes lopped to one side, especially while they narrow their eyes and lie in the sun.

Sweet gaze
Labradors sometimes like to look their loved ones in the eyes with a soft gaze, which can be a sign of love and affection.

Relaxed ears
When their ears are not lifted in an alert position or held back in a way that shows fear, but are neutral and relaxed, it shows they are calm and comfortable with you.

Head up

Labs can take a stance with their head held high that shows they are proud to be seen with you.

Down dog

This playful position with chest lowered, forearms bent, and butt in the air shows your pup is ready to play and have some fun with you.

Bouncy run

When your Lab is extra happy, they might jump around a lot when they run. It's so cute when they are too jumpy to contain their excitement!

Waggy tail

A wagging tail doesn't always mean a dog is happy. Sometimes dogs keep their tails low and wagging even when they are frightened or alert. But a high and fast wagging tail that goes along with other cheerful movements is a sure sign of a joyful pup.

Greetings

Walk time, for your Lab, is like a school or family reunion—the kind at which you're genuinely curious about people and stoked to see them after far too much time apart. It's a beautiful day in the neighborhood, and your Lab is so excited to say hello. They are also *pretty* confident that everybody is equally psyched to see them. In fact, people are probably out and about for the sole purpose of saying hello to your Labrador! I mean, what other reason would they have?

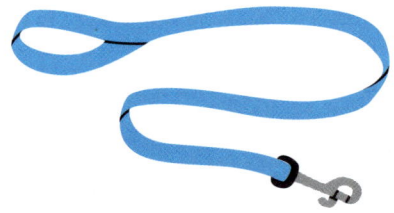

Puppies for Life

Labs are known for acting like a puppy for longer than other breeds. They tend to have a long puppyhood that lasts well past their adolescence. Not every Lab is the same, of course. Some Labs will be calm from day one, while others will be bouncing off the walls for years. Maturity will come eventually. Until then, you'll have a Lab looking for fun at all times of the day. Or maybe your Lab drank from the fountain of youth, and will still be playing fetch and running to greet everyone in sight well into their senior years!

EMPATHY

You're not imagining it: **Dogs feel for you.** They are in tune with their people and are a particularly empathetic breed. That's what makes them such great therapy dogs and emotional support dogs for people of all ages. Just like us, they feel a whole array of emotions—**joyful** or **sad,** anxious or depressed, comfortable or uncomfortable. When you are down, your Lab senses it and knows just the trick to **bring your spirits up,** whether it's warming your feet, licking your face, or wiggling their butt to make you smile.

Canine Therapists

It makes sense that Labradors make incredible therapy dogs in nursing homes, hospitals, mental health institutions, hospices, and schools. They have an instinctive desire to protect their people, and they can perceive our emotional states and provide comfort. They have evolved alongside us to read our emotions, the tones of our voices, and even the expressions on our faces for cues on how to respond. They can sense when we are happy, stressed, or upset.

Sometimes the presence of a Labrador is all you need to cheer you up. They will sit beside you, follow you around, and gaze up at you with kind, empathetic eyes and a sweet smile. They can offer love, comfort, and affection when their people need it most. Studies show that snuggling with your pup can have health benefits, such as lowering blood pressure and the stress hormone cortisol. Our pups experience health benefits too! Rubbing their bellies and giving them pats can stimulate the production of oxytocin and endorphins, or "happy hormones," for all! Labs will listen and offer no judgment or preconceived ideas about who you are supposed to be—attributes that we look for in a quality therapist. And you don't have to worry about whether they take your insurance!

Pack Animals

We used to think of wolf packs as vicious hierarchies, but more recent research has led to the understanding that they are just families looking out for one another. Experts who study wolf behavior see the leaders as parents who guide, teach, and care for their pack members. This collaborative instinct is demonstrated by Labrador behavior.

Dogs of breeds that are particularly social, including Labs, can feel what others are feeling. This comes from a deep-rooted instinct to protect the pack. Empathy serves pack animals well in the wild; it helps them keep each other safe. If there is a threat, fear spreads throughout the group, and the dogs stay close and move together, looking after one another so that no one is left behind. Their devotion and loyalty to one another will lead to the overall success of the pack.

When it comes to domesticated Lab pups, we are in the pack. Labradors trust their human companions to provide them with food, play, and love. This gives them a sense of belonging. In return, they are loyal and loving to us. We can form deep bonds with our Labradors that are unlike any other relationship. We couldn't ask for more!

There for You

A 2018 study from the scientifc journal, *Learning & Behavior,* shows that dogs react to human emotions and jump to the rescue when their companion is in distress. For the study, dog owners stood behind a glass door so their dogs could see and hear them, and they were told to either cry or hum. The dogs reacted three times faster to the crying, pushing through the door to "rescue" their owners. The dogs who responded to their human in distress showed lower levels of stress in their own response, which suggests they were not upset themselves, but motivated to react just by their empathy.

This study confirms what dog lovers feel in their hearts: Dogs have empathy. This is obvious when a Labrador comes to the rescue by bringing you a toy to cheer you up or gazing at you sweetly to show you they are with you and will do what it takes to let you know.

Needy

Labs are an extremely affectionate breed, but sometimes they can be a bit needy. They will follow you around the house, stare at you all hours of the day, and try to sit on your lap. Good news: Your Lab loves you and wants to spend time with you! Their neediness might be a part of their personality or could come from boredom or separation anxiety. Whatever the source, encourage more exercise and mental stimulation to support their independence and keep them away from unhealthy habits such as begging for your attention or chewing furniture. Ultimately, they just want to be near you. Their incredible attention to human needs and their sensitive nature means that we need to take special care of their emotional needs as well. Make sure to give them an affectionate pat—and include them on an outing when you can—to show them you love them just as much as they love you.

Keeping You Young

Labs are the perfect dogs for seniors. At a time in life during which you might feel more alone, your Lab will provide the companionship you need with a lick on the face, a cuddle, and a wagging tail. Studies have shown that people who own dogs are more likely to survive adverse health events such as heart attacks and strokes as they enjoy a longer and happier life. Loving a dog increases levels of oxytocin, dopamine, and serotonin–the happy hormones!

The Center for Disease Control and Prevention (CDC) recommends that adults over the age of 65 walk for about 150 minutes each week, and what is a better way to get outside than taking your Lab out for a jaunt? Dog owners tend to report getting thirty more minutes of exercise a day than their pet-less peers do. Your Lab won't let you slow down. Instead, they'll help relieve joint pain, strengthen your immune system, and, most importantly, boost your mood.

In the Spotlight

Labrador retrievers have been the dog of choice for a number of presidents and politicians, including Bill Clinton, Henry Kissinger, and former French president Jacques Chirac. The Clinton family's dog Buddy was a male chocolate Lab whose first public appearance was at the 1992 Democratic National Convention. He excitedly wagged his tail as his owner gave his acceptance speech for the nomination to be president of the United States.

The Lab was also the dog of choice for literary mavens such as Ernest Hemingway and Roald Dahl. Hemingway lovingly referred to his Lab as "Black Dog," and Black Dog accompanied the author as he wrote at the typewriter in the early morning, hunted lizards beside the pool when they lived in Cuba, and rested his chin on Hemingway's feet while he read in the evening.

Celebrities including Anne Hathaway, Arnold Schwarzenegger, Sylvester Stallone, Jessica Alba, Drew Barrymore, Reese Witherspoon, and Jennifer Garner have all owned and loved Labs. Reese Witherspoon revealed on Instagram that her black Lab pup, Major, had eaten her couch in a series of posts on Instagram. In a poll, she asked her followers, "Does this guy look like the culprit?"

Musicians such as Keith Richards, Paul McCartney, and Frank Sinatra were also a part of the club. McCartney recently rescued his black Lab Rose, but his previous black Lab puppy may have inspired the 1973 Wings song "Jet." (Though others think the song is referencing a horse.)

FAMILY
FRIENDS

It takes a **calm, patient, gentle dog** to tolerate the hustle and bustle and everyday noise of a family, and our **happy-go-lucky** Lab friends are up to the task. They are the perfect fun-time buddies, barking with delight and wagging their tails as they run alongside the kiddos in the park. They can also be **calm, still,** and **stoic.** Their protective nature and demeanor—broad heads and soft, slightly downturned, **intelligent eyes**—let the little ones know, "I've got your back, bud."

Baby Love

Labradors and toddlers have some similarities. They both like to pick up crumbs they find on the floor and give them a taste. They both crave our cuddles. And studies show that they operate at nearly the same level of intelligence. (More on this later!)

Because they relate so well to one another, toddlers and Labs can make for quite the dynamic duo. You might find your dog and toddler getting into some mischief together, falling asleep together, or even smoochy kissing when you turn your back. It's possible your Lab is actually licking applesauce off of your baby's cheeks, but that doesn't diminish the love they feel inside.

Boo Boos and Kisses

Labradors are very empathetic. The same qualities that make them great service dogs can help them nurture and protect your kids. When a kid goes boom and cries, Labs are *on it*. They will race over and attend to the clumsy little human with licks and snuggles. When you finally come running, they'll flash you a patronizing look as if to say, "Lucky for you I'm around."

Playmates

You can't hire your Labrador as a nanny, but they do make great playmates for the kids. Your kids and Lab can enjoy outdoor time together chasing a ball or romping in the grass. They can play hide and seek (the kid hides treats and the Labs seeks). You can enlist the kids in fun training activities to teach your Lab commands or have them set up an obstacle course to work on agility. When they all come inside after a backyard adventure, they'll make filthy little paw prints onto your floors, but hopefully they'll sleep well tonight. That is always the goal, right?

Patience

Labradors show a willingness to stand tall and strong and withstand the winds of a child's changing weathers. They've endured it all! They're used to getting swarmed by preschoolers with sticky fingers, getting poked and pulled, getting ridden like a horse, or being dressed up in a costume—like a unicorn Lab or Harry Potter Lab. Labs manage the chaos well with patient, tolerant, and gentle demeanors, seeming unflappable with their sturdy frames and smiling faces. They are more than pets—they are family members, and we love them so.

Marley & Me

The 2008 film *Marley & Me* was based on journalist John Grogan's book with the same name (which began as a column he'd written for *The Philadelphia Inquirer* documenting the life of his yellow Lab, Marley). The film starred Owen Wilson as John, Jennifer Aniston as his wife Jenny, and the dogs Jonah and Clyde as Marley.

Rumor has it that Clyde was just as mischievous and as full of life and spirit as the dog he played on screen. His pastimes included chewing and tearing up everything in sight, jumping into anything that could be perceived as a body of water, and eating whatever presented itself to him as food. While shooting one memorable scene in the film, Clyde went off script and peed on the coffee table. His trainer leapt after him, mortified, but the director thought it was genius and decided to keep that cut in the final version. And in typical Labrador fashion, Clyde was extremely motivated·by food. A little bit of ham-flavored baby food was dabbed on his costars' cheeks to entice Clyde to lick their faces.

SMARTIES

According to research done by dog expert Stanley Coren, Ph.D., the mental abilities of the average dog are close to those of a two- to two-and-a-half-year-old human child. **Smart dogs** can learn new commands, understand an average of 165 words, solve complex problems, count up to four or five, and dupe us to get treats. Out of all dog breeds, Labradors rank seventh in **intelligence,** which means they are considered one of the smartest dog breeds out there. (Border collies are number one.)

Now that we've determined that Labradors have the **smarts of a toddler,** you have to wonder . . . is there really any difference between the two? Basically not. You have to potty train them, feed them, exercise them, and pay for their medical expenses and toys. However, Labs won't grow out of their toddlerhood into a human who talks back when you tell them not to wear that crop top or that it's time to finish their homework. And while you might question some of their **life choices** when it comes to things like sniffing goose poop or sneaking a chicken bone out of the trash, you won't have to worry about them dating a deadbeat, borrowing your car, or asking you for money.

Adaptive Intelligence

Adaptive intelligence refers to a dog's ability to learn from their environment to solve problems on their own. Labradors are good at this! They can also learn to read our body language—they can pick up on subtle facial expressions such as our eyes being wide open or narrowed, and smiles or frowns. They can also learn by observation how to solve a puzzle toy, climb a fence, or con you into opening your palm and dropping some crumbs on the floor. Oh, they know they've got you wrapped around their little paw—one glance at that those big dewy eyes or that irresistible head tilt and you're toast.

Instinctive Intelligence

Instinctive intelligence refers to how dog breeds can instinctively perform the task they were bred to do: Herders herd, pointers point, guard dogs guard, and retrievers ... retrieve. Labradors, once again, are super intelligent in this way too! They were bred for their intelligence so they could help Newfoundland fisherman and hunters by bringing them game, and they were bred to be good companions too. Labradors also have a natural instinct to please. You can ask a lot of them, and they'll do it with a wag of the tail and a smile, just because they love you so.

Working and Obedience Intelligence

Dogs with high working and obedience intelligence are good at learning from humans. They are highly trainable and can learn to complete tasks and respond to our language. Labradors can be taught to bring you your shoes, open the door, find a lost item, and perform a myriad of other tasks. They can come to understand commands such as "sit," "stay," and "leave it" and adjust their behavior (especially if there's a meat snack in it for them). They might even understand some of what you're saying when you are gossiping, mansplaining, or repeating a story they've heard a million times. But don't worry—unless you're gabbing about snacks, squirrels, or playtime, your words won't concern them.

Tips for Keeping Dogs and Kids Safe

- Although they might be BFFs, it's still important to supervise a small child's interactions with a dog. Labradors can be jumpy and full of energy and excitement. A Lab's waggy tail can communicate a lot, but it can also be powerful enough to knock house plants, vases, and small kids to the floor.

- Teach kids how to respect a dog's privacy and limits. A dog's body language says a lot. Tail down, lots of yawns, lip licking, and averting the eyes are all signs the dog needs some space.

- Don't let your kiddos disturb the dog while he's eating or sleeping to prevent issues around guarding or privacy.

- Although it can be hard not to hug that big furry friend, it is important for kids to understand that hugs are not how most dogs, even Labs, like to receive affection. A scratch under the chin or a belly rub is a better, safer bet.

Thank You, Roger!

Roger, a failed drug dog, played an important role during a 2024 earthquake in eastern Asia. The yellow Lab looked for victims trapped or buried by rockslides following a 7.4 magnitude earthquake. Searching through a national park, Roger emerged as an unexpected star in the recovery operation. Before his career searching for people, Roger had failed out of customs drug-detection training for being too friendly and boisterous. Those found by Roger must be happy he failed out of school to be their hero.

Roger is famous for his service after such a treacherous and tragic time, but fame didn't change him (at one news conference, he gnawed on a microphone). Roger retired at nine years old in 2024.

DUCK
HUNTERS

Along with being extremely **happy-go-lucky, silly, friendly,** and **sociable,** Labradors have a natural game-finding and -retrieving ability, and a strong prey drive. As early as the 1830s, St. John's water dogs would bring Newfoundland fishermen the fish that had slipped from their hooks. Later, Labradors worked alongside hunters to retrieve ducks and other waterfowl. Bred to have **"soft mouths,"** they could keep the prey intact by holding it in their mouth without clamping down too hard and deliver it to their human. They were born to retrieve, and so retrieve they will!

Bird Dogs

When a bird has the nerve to fly into your Labrador's line of vision, their prey instincts will kick in. Your pup's ears will perk up, their body will stiffen, their eyes will flash with images of the catch, and they'll sprint off. Now, if you are a hunter, you might appreciate your "bird dog" or "gun dog" dropping a dead pheasant at your feet like a wrapped gift. But a bird carcass before our morning coffee might not be the gift a lot of us were hoping for. It is the thought that counts, though.

Gift Givers

Even if your Lab doesn't go after birds, they may still like to retrieve stray items from around the house to bring to their loved ones. They'll trot over to you with something random or indecipherable—balled up socks, a deflated football, the television remote, a chewed-up electric bill, your cell phone, something greenish, something damp, something furry—in their mouth and drop it at your feet … sorry. *Ew*. But be mindful that they think they've done a really good thing and will be anticipating your inevitable praise with their head held high. "You're welcome," they are trying to say.

Go Fetch

Fetch is another way for our Labs to put their retrieval instincts to good use, and it can be meditative and fun for both you and them. If it was up to your Labrador, you would be playing fetch for hours on end. Fetch all day, from sunrise to sundown! Maybe you had other plans, such as going to work or sleeping. Well, think again! Your pup is at your feet with a ball in their mouth.

But don't feel bad if your Lab is not really into fetch. Some dogs didn't get the memo about their DNA, and that's okay. If this is the case, they might do one of the following:

- Look up at you after you've thrown the ball with complete bafflement or indifference.

- Expect you to do the heavy lifting—fetch the ball for them yourself and drop it at their feet.

- Run off into the woods with the ball, never to return.

If the last option describes your dog, you might want to look into getting a fence.

Need for Speed

Labs are sporting dogs for more than their heightened senses. They can run up to 12 miles per hour (19 kph) within 3 seconds of starting. And they can even run up to 20 miles per hour (32 kph)! That's almost as fast as Usain Bolt. With the right training and a healthy diet, some Labs can reach 30 miles per hour (48 kph).

Of course, Labs are no match for the Greyhound, which can run up to 45 miles per hour (72 kph). But if you're out hunting or running around the yard, you may be shocked by your Lab's speed. If you try to outrun your Lab, you'll surely lose.

Smell

We rely on Labs for many things, including their keen sense of smell. Bred to be hunting dogs, tracking animals is in their blood. They also use their sense of smell to locate people in search and rescue missions, with the ability to find people literally buried under piles of rubble. They can be trained to track fugitives as well, learning to sniff out anything associated with the person's scent such as their clothes or other belongings. Once the Lab has the scent, they're on the trail!

What Is Prey Drive?

When we talk about dog breeds that have a strong prey drive, we usually mean they have an ancient genetic predisposition to pursue and capture prey—and some breeds are more designed to do this. Prey drive motivates dogs to bring their "captured prey" back to their owner. They are also considered to be higher energy dogs that want to work.

Of course, every dog is an individual with their own motivations, personalities, and desires. Although Labradors as a breed have a strong prey drive, there are a lot of factors that determine how strong this drive really is, including their breeding and environmental factors. A high-energy dog with a strong prey drive will not necessarily have aggressive tendencies. Although your pup might always have the urge to go after that rabbit, training them with positive reinforcement and simple commands such as "come," "stay," and "leave it" will teach them to stay focused on you and ignore things that catch their eye. There are also a lot of positives to having a dog with a strong prey drive. They are usually high-energy exercise partners, fun to play with, and easy to train.

Born for This

Some say that "if you love what you do, you'll never work a day in your life"—that's how Labs feel about hunting. Even if you don't love the outdoors, there are plenty of ways to reinforce your Lab's instincts.

Starting in their puppy years, you can give your Lab twenty minutes of "hunt training" every day. Your Lab can chase a sock around the house, find a hidden item once you've given them a scent, and be taught to lie down low as if to avoid being spotted by ducks. During these exercises, your Lab can learn to sit and stay before their search or walk at your heel (which can also come in handy when you encounter any person or animal who makes you wary).

Your Lab deserves an abundance of praise for their successes, but sometimes there is no need for treats. They hunt and play for the joy of it because it is what they were born to do.

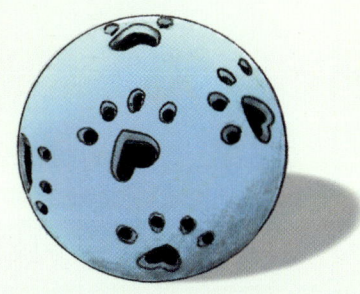

Don't Let Your Pup Be the Boss!

- **Start early.** Begin training your dog early on in their life, when they are between eight and twelve weeks of age. This will create good habits and make your life together much more fulfilling. This early training is also wonderful for bonding.

- **Always reward good behavior.** Train your Lab with positive reinforcements such as treats, praise, and quality time. They will understand your expectations and learn good habits. Especially when it comes to training your Lab for the outdoors, a quick treat immediately after they respond to a cue will help them learn.

- **Socialize your Lab!** Labs are social dogs, and they need early experiences mixing with new people and dogs so they learn to play well with others. The more exposed they are to everyday sights and sounds—the car, doorbells, crowds, other rowdy puppies, and the like—the easier their training will be. Arrange controlled meetings with others so your Lab can learn to handle any situation with grace.

- **The power of exercise and mental stimulation.**
  Labs will chew on anything. Their destructive chewing
  or excessive barking can easily be redirected with
  a toy or praise when they're calm and collected.
  Exercise can curb this behavior as well; provide at
  least thirty minutes a day on the leash or off. Even a
  hide and seek game in the house using toys or treats
  mentally engages your Lab.

EATING
MACHINES

We know that Labs are blessed with many skills and talents—including **retrieving, game hunting, swimming, cuddling,** and so much more—but if there's one thing that Labradors excel at, it's eating. In fact, twenty-five percent of purebred Labradors have a genetic mutation that causes them to be hungry all the time and prevents them from feeling full when they have had enough. Dogs with this genetic predisposition also burn fewer calories from the food they eat, and they are susceptible to obesity, which can put a strain on their heart, hips, and joints.

Labradors are not overly fussy or discerning when it comes to their palate. Not at all. They will put pretty much **anything** and **everything** into their mouths, whether or not it is actually **"edible."** Hopefully you will be spared having to take them to the ER to surgically remove foreign objects from their gullet. Lab owners know they have to keep an eye on their pups; be prepared to **dog-proof** your place, train your pup to **"leave it,"** and make sure not to leave that charcuterie platter at snout level.

Scavengers

A Lab owner knows the particular excitement of trying to pry a foreign object from their dog's mouth. On a stroll on a seemingly uneventful afternoon, things can turn fast. You glance away for just one instant, and the next thing you know, your Lab is gnawing on something unusual. What is it? A rock? Moldy pizza? A beach ball? You shout, "Leave it!" but you can almost see it going down their throat as they swallow the object whole. You can then see the shape of it on the abdominal x-ray, and now you've spent what it would have cost you to fly to Europe to have it removed.

Counter Surfers

Your Lab wants to please and will do just about anything for you and really wants to do the right thing—but if you leave an egg sandwich, stick of butter, leftover pasta, or bowl of fruit on the counter, we all know how this story is going to end.

Garbage Hounds

It's not just about the food that's right in front of your Lab. The enticing smells of discarded food scraps and leftovers are calling to them from that bin under the sink. Once they paw or nose their way in there, they'll find all sorts of goodies: chicken bones, empty soup cans, fast food wrappers, coffee grounds, banana peels, and egg shells ... and will likely cause tummy troubles at best.

Your Lab's Favorite Foods

- **Protein:** Chicken, turkey, eggs, and beef all have a ton of amino acids, which will support your Lab's body functions and strength. Protein will provide energy, help build and repair muscles, and support skin and hair growth.

- **Dog foods with fatty acids and calcium:** These vital ingredients will make your Lab's skin, coat, bones, and teeth healthy. A healthy body starts with a rounded meal.

Tips for Managing Your Hunger Machine

- Train your Labrador a "leave it" command so they'll drop miscellaneous items they've scavenged.

- Keep a lid on the trashcan to stop your garbage hound from getting into trouble.

- Make sure to keep your Lab's body moving to prevent boredom-grazing.

- Labs are incredibly intelligent and can work around obstructions to break into the kibble. They'll find a solution, such as using their noses or paws to open the fridge, pantry, or garbage bin. Seal and lock up bags of food—you might even need a padlock.

- Keep enticing plants and other potential edible items out of your Lab's reach.

- Don't give in to those puppy eyes! If you've given your Labrador their regular meals, they will manage just fine without your table scraps.

- If you have a garbage hound, keep your pup's environment free of small items they could eat to prevent trips to the ER.

- If you notice your Lab likes to munch on things that could make them sick, take them to the vet to rule out health issues such as hypothyroidism and to make sure they are not lacking any nutrients they need.

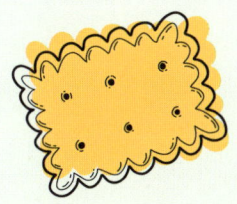

AT YOUR SERVICE

Labradors make some of the **best service dogs** because they are **calm, loving, gentle, empathetic, friendly, determined to work,** and **eager to please.** Labs can help people in many ways, including alerting people with **hearing loss** to the phone or doorbell, providing deep pressure therapy to those who need **mobility assistance,** and stopping children from running into the road. They also possess a **confidence** that many other breeds don't; Labs are naturally **social** and will approach people to provide assistance, a quality that is necessary in a service dog.

Guide Dogs

As guide dogs, Labs can help owners with low vision or blindness navigate the world. These companions work as a team with their owner to find an unobstructed path to walk. They lead their owner to their destination—their workplace, school, train station, or anywhere else. These Labs live with "puppy raisers" who take special care of future guide dogs, take them to puppy training classes, teach the puppies general commands, and keep them happy and healthy. Lab puppies then start the rigorous eighteen-month training process when they are six months old.

Less than five percent of dogs are cut out for this kind of work. They can be kicked out of the program for issues including a lack of confidence, health problems, appearance, preferences for only certain people, and the list goes on. Guide dog dropouts shouldn't feel bad about themselves, though. Don't let them lose heart. Call it a career change, a new lease on life, a fresh start, a new beginning! Plus, there's a long waiting list to adopt "career-change dogs" because they are often so healthy, calm, confident, and sweet.

Heart Help

Cardiac Alert Dogs use their strong sense of smell to recognize chemical alterations that occur when their owner's blood pressure or heart rate changes. They can also use their incredible sense of hearing to detect variations in breathing or heart rate changes. If they notice a change, they are trained to alert their owner by pawing at them, nudging them, and barking. They can also use their bodies to break their owner's fall, help them open and close drawers to get what they need, run over to them with medication, and even paw a button on the phone programmed to dial 911.

Pep the Prison Dog

It may sound surprising, but a black Lab was put behind bars for bad behavior at the historic Pennsylvania Eastern State Penitentiary.

Pep arrived on August 31, 1924, got his mug shot, and was given an official intake number (C-2559). His name was entered into the ledger as "A Dog."

What was his crime? Murder.

Just kidding. Overcrowding had led to low morale among the incarcerated, and the governor of Pennsylvania sent Pep to live at the prison to serve as a happy remedy. The hope was that the presence of a loving and joyful Labrador might be a source of comfort for the inmates, brightening their moods, which might, in turn, shorten their sentences.

Of course, the public was outraged by this slanderous incrimination and letters of complaint from Pennsylvania to the Philippines arrived at the penitentiary. Ultimately, though, Pep lived a full life bringing happiness to inmates. Today, there are programs that bring animals into correctional institutions such as New Leash on Life USA, a nonprofit dedicated to improving the lives of many by teaching them to care for and socialize shelter dogs. Cultivating a powerful bond between humans and dogs can bring hope, healing, and well-being to all.

Psychiatric Service Dogs

Labradors are also incredible psychiatric service dogs, assisting people with anxiety and mood disorders including autism spectrum disorder, ADHD, and OCD. They are trained to seek support if their owner is unwell, and they learn commands that can help their owner in emergency situations. They can retrieve medication or a phone. They can sense shifts in their owner's mental state by smelling microscopic changes in hormone levels and can offer comfort and support by nuzzling and licking to calm their owner down. They can be trained to help distract someone who is stuck in an obsessive loop by pawing at them or fetching them a dog brush or remote. They can block other people, staying close by in public to protect an owner who has difficulty interacting with others. They can also provide Deep Pressure Therapy (DPT) by lying on their owner's chest, providing warmth and comfort to help settle them down.

Bed Bug Dogs

Did you know about this one? Although beagles are one of the best breeds to sniff out bed bugs because of their incredible sense of smell, our Labrador buddies are also commonly used to detect those pesky pests. They are ten thousand to one hundred thousand times more sensitive to odors than an average human. They can sniff out the bugs and eggs in mattresses, walls, and couches (*yuck!*) in early stages to prevent a full-on infestation, and they are quick at the job.

Dog of the Millennium

A male yellow Lab named Endal (1995–2009) came to his owner's rescue when it counted most. Allen Parton suffered head injuries while serving in the Gulf War, leaving him unable to speak or write and affecting his ability to recognize and communicate with his family. Endal nearly didn't qualify to work as a service dog due to his own injuries. He had osteochondrosis in both front legs, a condition that affects joints. Luckily, he got the job anyway. He became Allen's reliable and devoted companion, helping him with day-to-day tasks such as pressing the emergency button on a phone to get help when necessary, assisting with shopping, and even unloading the dishwasher.

One day in 2001, Endal came to Allen's rescue after Allen was knocked out of his wheelchair by a passing car. Endal pulled Allen into a recovery position, retrieved his phone from beneath the car, pulled out a blanket from the wheelchair and covered Allen, and went looking for help at a nearby hotel. The story went viral.

Endal became "the most decorated dog in the world," winning awards such as "Dog of the Millennium" and the PDSA Gold Medal for Animal Gallantry and Devotion to Duty. He rose to fame as possibly the most famous assistance dog in the United Kingdom.

OUTDOORSMEN

If you're looking for a friend to join you on outdoor adventures, your Labrador has got your back! Labs are **hearty, strong, bold,** and **brave,** and their webbed feet make them natural swimmers. They'll hike up the mountain with you all day and then snuggle in beside you in a tent to keep you warm. They'll retrieve that ball out of the mucky river over and over again. They'll run beside you on the beach, sand on their nose, drenched in salty water. They'll **keep you company** on any excursion you've got planned. If there's a chance for them to move their bodies, get outside, and be with you, they are game. It's a win-win for everyone!

Hikers

Labradors are the best hiking buds. They have great endurance for climbing all day, especially if there's fetch involved. After a nice long day out in the forest, your dog will be barking, but at least they will be content. Labs have a can-do attitude that keeps them going and inspires us all. (Just make sure not to overdo it and keep them hydrated!)

Swimmers

Labradors are built for the water with their webbed toes, long legs, and water-repellent coats. Keep a towel handy because they will be enticed by any water—the ocean, a lake, a frozen pond, a bog, a creek, a river, a mucky marsh, a puddle, or even the neighbor's kiddie pool. Before you can say Nancy, your Lab will be up to their neck in water, bobbing after that stick. If fetch is involved, forget about it.

Now, having said that, it's also true that not *all* Labradors are good swimmers. Some dogs don't really care about what they were "bred" to do. While some fancy themselves aquaphiles, others prefer to stand on the shoreline and watch everyone else splash around while they bark their heads off.

Anatomy of a Lab

Labs come from Newfoundland, Canada, where they were bred to withstand tough work and invigorating sport.

- **Nose:** Labs have a great sense of smell, and this is put to the test when retrieving ducks. It also helps when looking for squirrels in the backyard.

- **Webbed feet:** Labs have webbed toes, and they can swim like a fish. Labs are great swimmers, their webbed paws acting as snowshoes in colder climates.

- **Coat:** To survive the tough Canadian winters, Labs developed thick, water-resistant fur and strong bones. This lets them withstand extreme temperatures and swim competently. Their strong bones and muscles account for their agility and speed.

- **Brain:** Labs can be easily trained if you're willing to do the work. As the preferred breed for guide and service dogs, Labs are clearly predisposed to learn commands, be loyal, and keep your best interest at heart.

Campers

There's something about being with a dog that makes you appreciate your surroundings even more. When we are with them, we can truly savor all that nature offers. We can see the excitement of the world through their eyes—the sound of the birds, the smells of animal urine, and the sight of critters who'd better *watch it*. Dogs make the best camping companions. Of course, you'll need to plan ahead and bring supplies such as dog food, water, treats, bowls, leash and collar or harness, portable kennel or stake and tether line, portable pet bed, toys, and a first-aid kit. But it will be worth it! There's nothing like a Labrador trotting beside you in the forest, lying with you by the campfire under the starry sky, and snuggled up beside you in your tent as you both snore your cares away.

Otter Tails and Twizzles

A Labrador's tail acts as a kind of powerful rudder and propeller to help them move about in the water. According to the official American Kennel Club (AKC) Labrador breed standard, "the tail should be free from feathering and clothed thickly all around with the Labrador's short, dense coat, thus having that peculiar rounded appearance that has been described as the 'otter' tail." Also, "it may be carried gaily, but should not curl over the back." In addition, the ideal standard of the breed has what's called a "twizzle tail," meaning that the hair on their tail should swirl, "wrapping" around the tail.

Let's remember, though, we're talking about the gold standard of appearance here. We'll love our pups unconditionally, cute quirks and all—and with or without an otter tail or a twizzle tail!

Colors of Labs

The AKC recognizes three official colors for Labs—black, chocolate, and yellow. Labs also come in beautiful variations of those shades, including charcoal, silver, champagne, and white, and all have become popular amongst breeders and families.

Black

Historically, black was the most common color in early breeding lines. The breed's roots traced back to St. John's water dogs, which were all black with white markings on their chest and paws. Black Labs were the classic breed standard until yellow and chocolate became more prevalent.

Brown or Chocolate

Over time, as the breeding process diversified, chocolate Labs became more popular and widely available. The brown coats are a recessive trait, meaning a chocolate Lab puppy must have two parents who both carry the gene.

Yellow

Yellow Labs developed thanks to a different genetic marker, which effectively turns the black or brown coloring off. Yellow has now become a breed standard and comes in a wide range of shades, from pale cream to buff (which is darker than cream but still on the lighter side) to fox red. Today, the yellow Labrador is the most popular color with a strong presence in the media and popular culture.

(Of course, all Labs are sweet love bugs no matter their coat color!)

AFFECTION

There's nothing quite like licks from a Lab. **Empathetic, friendly,** and **ready to love,** Labradors have a **sweet** and **easy** nature that makes them the perfect companions. Labradors are not shy in the least about showing their **affection.** When they love, they love *hard*. When they are excited to see you, they will let you know. They'll move and shake their bodies, vigorously wag their tails, climb into your lap, and drench you in slobber. They **adore you** and want you to know. Luckily for them, we feel just the same!

Slobber Monsters

Your Labrador might think you are a human lollipop. Licking is their way of showing you they are submissive and friendly and mean you no harm. It's a comfort response that reminds them of when they were puppies and their mama used to lick their fur. Ah, those were the days. Labradors lick to groom us. They lick us when they are anxious or scared to calm themselves down. They lick to say hello, goodbye, thank you, and "I love you more than you'll ever know."

Alarm Clocks

Maybe you are still fast asleep when morning comes, but your Labrador thinks you'd better get up. It's hard to believe you have both had to endure eight hours of shut-eye, as in eight whole hours without snuggling or playing fetch! Now, the sun is rising and the day is young. You'll be awoken with face licks and some wild dance moves and spinnies to get you going. Life is good. Labradors are here to remind us of that.

Pouncers

Labradors can be a little bit like Tigger from
Winnie-the-Pooh. Prepare to be sniffed and tackled
by your furry friend when you walk into the room.
How can they be expected to hold it all in when it's
you? *You!* Will anyone else in your life give that kind
of a reception? Does it take coaxing for the humans in
your life to get up off the couch when you arrive?
This is the thing about dogs! They make us feel
loved and adored. They just want to be with you,
and there's nothing wrong with that.

Gazers

Labradors are not shy about looking you in the eye.
They will stare at you to get your attention, to try to
interpret your body language and connect with
you, and to show you they feel connected to you.
Maybe you're busy paying bills, eating breakfast, or
talking on the phone ... that's okay with them.
Take a moment to pause and feel the presence
of a pup gazing fondly at you with a smile.

Ringo and Ol' Blue Eyes

Frank Sinatra rescued and adopted many stray animals over the years and was particularly fond of his pups. When his daughter asked him where heaven is, he replied, "Heaven is where all the animals go." Photographer John Dominis captured lots of loving images of Sinatra with his dog Ringo, who looks to be a yellow Lab mix. There are images of Sinatra relaxing at home, reading with his feet on the coffee table while Ringo sits beside him. In another photo, Sinatra sits by the piano with Ringo's paws in his hands as if they're dancing together. And in another he holds Ringo's face, the two of them gazing at one another with adoration. I mean, come on now. Could this be any sweeter?

Lap Dogs

Who says you have to be able to fit in someone's lap in order to be a lap dog? Though your Labrador might be somewhere between 55 and 80 pounds (25 and 36 kg), they will plop down on you to be as close to you as they can. Just as some small dogs have big dog syndrome, many Labs seem to think they're a Pomeranian or bichon frise. Take it as a compliment! It means you make them feel safe. Your legs might fall asleep after a little while, but that's a small price to pay for love.

Oldest Lab

The average lifespan of a Lab is ten to twelve years old, but Bella of Derbyshire, England, far exceeded expectations. Born in 1979, Bella lived to be twenty nine years old. She was even recorded by the *Guiness World Records*. In 1982, Bella was adopted by owners, David and Daisy. She went on to enjoy her long life in the beautiful hills of Derbyshire, where her favorite pastime was sniffing around in the garden.

The oldest dog to have *ever* lived *might* have been an Australian cattle dog named Bluey, who lived to be thirty years old. Sadly, her owner lost her paperwork, so she couldn't make it official.

Lovers

Labrador retrievers have been popular across the world for so long because they are truly the cream of the crop. They are always eager to please, there to serve, friendly to everyone they meet, and ready to love. They are affectionate and have winning personalities and kind souls. They are our friendly faces, our empathetic souls, our family friends, our smarties, our retrievers, our outdoor adventurers, our sweet and easygoing companions. They are our Labradors.

Finding the Perfect Name for Your Labrador Retriever

If you're considering a Labrador retriever for yourself and ruminating on baby names, here's a list of names that might strike your fancy.

Acorn	Biscuit	Champ	Darcy
Alex	Blaze	Chance	Dolly
Alfie	Blue	Charlie	Dot/Dottie
Amber	Brian	Chase	Ducky
Archer	Brie	Chip	Duke
Ash	Bronco	Cinder	Echo
Aspen	Brooks	Cliff	Ellie
Bailey	Bruce	Clover	Emmett
Baxter	Bruno	Cole	Finnigan
Bean	Buck	Coco	Fudge
Bear	Buddy	Cookie	Gill
Beau	Butter	Cooper	Ginger
Bella	Callie	Daisy	Goose
Birdie	Cedar	Dakota	Gracie

Gunnar	Luna	Onyx	Rocky
Guppy	Mac	Opal	Roman
Hank	Maggie	Oreo	Rover
Harry	Mateo	Owen	Ruby
Harvey	Marley	Parker	Rusty
Hawk	Mason	Peanut	Sadie
Hazel	Maverick	Pearl	Sally
Hershey	Max	Penny	Scout
Holden	Millie	Pepper	Sebastian
Honey	Milo	Piper	Siobhan
Hudson	Moby	Poppy	Smudge
Hunter	Mocha	Pumpkin	Spike
Iris	Molly	Raider	Stella
Jersey	Moose	Ranger	Sugar
Jet	Murphy	Raven	Sunny
Kai	Nala	Ray	Teddy
Koda	Nelly	Rebel	Tucker
Lake	Nemo	Red	Waffles
Lily	Neptune	Reese	Whiskey
Levi	Nora	Rex	Willow
Lucky	Nova	River	Winnie
Lulu	Olive	Robin	Zoe

Taking Care of Your Labrador

Health Considerations

- Labrador retrievers are generally healthy and can live long and happy lives. Breeders should screen for conditions including obesity, joint issues, ear infections, eye conditions, hereditary myopathy, and exercise induced collapse (EIC). Labradors can also develop a life-threatening condition called bloat.

- When you're looking for a Lab to complete your family, be sure to find a reputable breeder and take your Lab to routine vet visits to keep them healthy.

Recommended Health Tests from the National Breed Club

- Hip Evaluation

- Progressive Retinal Atrophy, PRCD (PRA-prcd, PRCD) DNA Test

- Exercise-Induced Collapse (EIC) DNA Test

- D Locus (Dilute) DNA Test

- Centronuclear Myopathy (CNM) DNA Test

- Elbow Evaluation

- Ophthalmologist Evaluation

Breed Information from the AKC:

akc.org/dog-breeds/labrador-retriever/

The Labrador Retriever Club Mission Statement

thelabradorclub.com/mission-statement/

Grooming

- Brush your Lab daily or weekly, depending on how much they shed. Their water-repellant double coat sheds a lot.

- Bathe your Lab occasionally, especially after outdoor romps.

- Trim their nails and brush their teeth.

- Check their ears, eyes, and nose for infection.

- Wipe their feet to prevent smelly paws.

Exercise

- Labradors require a great deal of exercise to stay happy, healthy, and well-behaved. If Labs don't get enough exercise, they are more likely to become hyperactive or destructive, so it's imperative to take the time to tire them out. They love swimming, dock diving, running, and retrieving.

- Agility and obedience training can also help to keep them mentally and physically stimulated.

Training

- Labradors are incredibly friendly and social and can be wonderful additions to any household, but they do need training to keep them from developing bad habits.

- These medium- to large-sized dogs can be boisterous, jumping up on strangers, bolting through the door, or getting overexcited. It's important to expose your Lab puppy to a variety of scenarios, locations, people, and pets to help them learn social skills. Early obedience training will help you manage any difficult behavior that your Lab is beginning to develop.

- With training and attention, Labradors can grow into well-mannered and well-adjusted adults, and they will become an integral and loving part of the family.

Nutrition

- A Labrador retriever should eat a protein-rich, low-carbohydrate, high-quality diet with veterinarian guidance to meet your dog's specific needs.

- Many Labradors have a genetic mutation that makes them hungry while preventing them from feeling full, and they also burn twenty five percent less energy than dogs without this mutation.

- Nearly a quarter of Labs are prone to obesity, which can affect their heart and joints. Your Lab's calorie consumption and weight should be monitored, and while treats can be a good reinforcement for training exercises, they should be given in moderation.

- Make sure to research which human foods are safe for Labradors and which ones are not, and always contact your vet with any questions about weight or diet.

Labrador Resources

The AKC Marketplace website offers resources for purchasing Labrador retriever puppies from a breeder. According to AKC, "AKC Marketplace is the only site to exclusively list 100% AKC puppies from AKC-Registered litters and the breeders who have cared for and raised these puppies are required to follow rules and regulations established by the AKC."

marketplace.akc.org/puppies/labrador-retriever

Labrador Retriever Club, Inc.

"The goal of the Club shall be to encourage and promote quality in the breeding and performance of pure-bred Labrador Retrievers and to do all possible to bring their natural attributes as working retrievers to perfection."

thelabradorclub.com

Peak Lab Rescue

"Peak Lab Rescue is a community of like-minded individuals working together to end dog homelessness in North Carolina. We are the largest foster-based dog rescue in the state. Our mission is to save Lab Mixes and other dogs in need from abuse, neglect, abandonment, and high-kill shelters throughout NC."

peaklabrescue.com

Acknowledgments

I would like to thank my editor, Nicole James, for her vision and enthusiasm, as well as Sarah O'Connor and the whole team at Quarto for helping to bring this series of books about dogs to life. Thanks to my friends and readers of my work over the years, fellow artists in the Cut and Paste ARIM (Artist Residency in Motherhood), my writing teachers at Sarah Lawrence College, Tufts, and Friends School. Thank you to my close friends who have been there, always, supporting my writing. You know who you are. Thanks to my childhood dog, Sparky, and to my sweet and silly Sato dog, Cali, who makes us laugh and brings us endless joy and love. Thank you to the hard working volunteers at Heaven Can Wait Rescue - Northstar Dogs for Adoption for bringing Cali to us. Finally, I would like to thank my family: my parents, Jan and Michael, and my sister, Rachel; my nieces, aunts, uncles, cousins, and in-laws. I'm forever grateful to my husband, Kevin, for his kindness, love, and support, and to my incredible daughters, Nora and Rosie, who will always have my heart.

About the Author

Sara Weiss holds an MFA from Sarah Lawrence College. She is the author of *A Frenchie Life*, *A Golden Life,* and *The Totally Awesome World of Caitlin Clark*. Her writing has appeared in journals and magazines such as *Literary Mama*, *Mutha*, *Lilith*, *Waterwheel Review*, *Bustle,* and *Brain Child*, among others. She has written audio scripts for *Good Night Stories for Rebel Girls* and works as a college writing consultant. She lives in the Hudson Valley with her husband, two daughters, and their little Sato rescue dog named Cali.

Who Can Have Just One Dog?

With so many breeds to love, collect and enjoy all the companion titles celebrating our favorite friends:

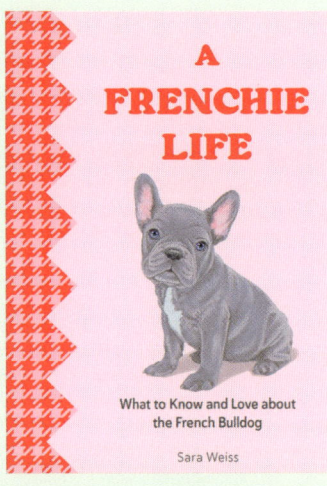

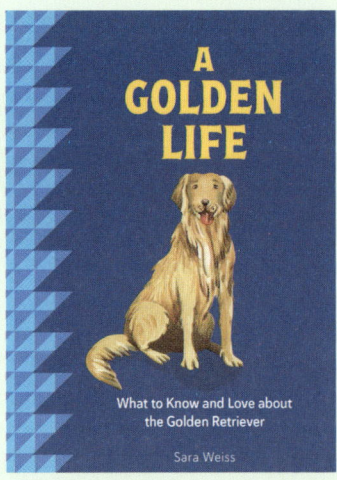

A Frenchie Life

What to Know and Love about the French Bulldog

ISBN: 978-1-57715-503-4

A Golden Life

What to Know and Love about the Golden Retriever

ISBN: 978-1-57715-502-7